Walking the Way of the Cross

Prayers for Your Personal Journey

John Elliston

WALKING THE WAY OF THE CROSS
Prayers for Your Personal Journey

Copyright © 2005 John P. Elliston
Original edition published in English under the title WALKING THE WAY OF THE CROSS by Kevin Mayhew Ltd, Buxhall, England.
This edition copyright © Fortress Press 2019

All rights reserved. Except for brief quotations in critical articles or reviews, no part of this book may be reproduced in any manner without prior written permission from the publisher. Email copyright@augsburgfortress.org or write to Permissions, Fortress Press, PO Box 1209, Minneapolis, MN 55440-1209.

Scripture quotations are from *The Revised Standard Version of the Bible*, copyright © 1946, 1952 and 1971 by the Division of Christian Education of the National Council of Churches in the USA. Used by permission.

Cover image: Photo by asoggetti on Unsplash
Cover design: Lauren Williamson

Print ISBN: 978-1-5064-5970-7

CONTENTS

About the Author		4
Introduction		7
1.	Jesus Is Condemned to Death	9
2.	Jesus Takes up His Cross	11
3.	Jesus Falls the First Time	13
4.	Jesus Meets His Loving Mother	15
5.	Simon Helps Jesus Carry His Cross	17
6.	Veronica Wipes the Face of Jesus	19
7.	Jesus Falls a Second Time	21
8.	Jesus Meets the Weeping Women	23
9.	Jesus Falls a Third Time	25
10.	Jesus Is Stripped of His Garments	27
11.	Jesus Is Nailed to the Cross	29
12.	Jesus Dies upon the Cross	31
13.	Jesus Is Taken Down from the Cross	33
14.	Jesus Is Laid in the Tomb	35
15.	The Resurrection	37

About the Author

The Reverend Dr. John Elliston is a Baptist minister, currently working at Grange Road Baptist Church in Darlington, England. He has written a number of books of prayers including *Here in our Midst*, *Footprints on Sand*, *From the Depths*, *From the Foot of the Cross*, and *Walking With Pain*.

*You call us to follow you,
to let go of all attachment,
to surrender our lives in love,
to walk the Way of the Cross.*

Introduction

Lord, as I walk the Way of the Cross,
walk with me,
for the load I carry bears down upon my back
and I fear I will not reach the end.
I need to tell someone of the pain and grief
that threatens at times to overwhelm me,
the pity and the anger that I feel
when tragedy again touches lives
that are already scarred by tears,
and the aching sense of helplessness
that comes when I try to pray.
I want to speak of my loneliness
within the absurdity of your calling,
of the times of darkness, and of those moments
when the cost of caring seems just too much.
I want you to know, Lord, but more than that,
I want you to walk the Way with me,
because as I walk toward my death
I am more frightened than anyone knows.

1

Jesus Is
Condemned to Death

We do not choose death. We know neither the time nor the manner of its coming, but we know that sentence has been passed upon all humanity and death is inevitable.

> *For as in Adam all die, so also in Christ shall all be made alive.* 1 Corinthians 15:22

Lord, confronted by the truth of death, I am afraid.
Apprehension fills my body like an arctic chill;
an icy, penetrating shadow on the life that's left.
Fear paralyzes my spirit,
and the love, the faith,
and the sheer glory of the life you have given me
cry out, "I am not ready to die . . . I am unprepared."
Yet suddenly, now, I know that my time has come,
and even though it is a time not of my choosing,
I must accept that it is so and walk the path of my
   destiny.

Holy Father, come to me now in Christ,
so that as I prepare to leave this world
that has been my home,
I may have wisdom to discern what is still of value

John Elliston

and what is not;
insight to distinguish the real treasure
from what is ephemeral;
and vision to prevent the deeper truths of life
from becoming submerged under a sea of distraction.

May I, on this my final journey, hold on by faith
to those things that my pilgrimage has taught me:

> that love is stronger than death,
> that hope transcends the boundaries of flesh,
> and that to hold Christ
> is to hold everything that matters.

Amen.

2

Jesus Takes up His Cross

There is an ambiguity at the heart of the gospel story. It arises because the writers of the New Testament constantly try to hold together both the chosen-ness of the Cross and the idea that Jesus' walk to the Cross was the enforced journey of a condemned man. The presence of this ambiguity only makes sense if the Way of the Cross is interpreted through love; Christ did not choose the Cross, he chose love: the Cross was what love cost.

Lord, the more deeply I become involved in the world
and the more intensely concerned I become
for the lives of others,
the more violent becomes the inner challenge,
the more intensely I feel their pain,
and the more certain becomes the shackle of no
  retreat.
I did not know, but I now understand what you
  meant
when you denied to your disciples the backward look.
For, like the path of the plow,
the Way allows no compromise;
like the cup of suffering, it must be drunk entire,
and like a road to execution, it allows me no escape.

John Elliston

Lord, the weight that I bear in this world
is not the weight of my execution:
it is the weight of love;

it is the weight of emotional care and concern
for those that suffer,
it is the weight of responsibility
for those whose humanity I share,
it is the weight of other people's pain
that drains my strength.

But having once accepted the load,
I fear I cannot bear it.
My anxiety, my pain, my exhaustion,
press me to the ground.

Grant me the strength to believe that,
as you are beside me as I bear my cross,
so you are beneath me, sharing the load.

Amen.

3

Jesus Falls the First Time

O Lord, heal me, for my bones are troubled. My soul also is sorely troubled. But thou, O Lord— how long? Psalm 6:2–3

For Jesus the way of the cross was a desert road, and the load that he carried the tool of execution. For me, the desert is within, and the load that I carry is doubt, despair, and fear.

Lord, I have fallen,
and the taunting crowd taunt me as they taunted you,
mocking my God, undermining my faith,
stealing the dignity of my faltering belief.
But not for me
the dry dust of earth meeting an exhausted body;
not for me the dead weight of the gibbet to crush
   my spine;
not for me the inner struggle to sustain my love,
nor limp limbs that will not do my bidding—
for I have fallen,
not on the outer road
that links the palace of Pilate

to the Place of the Skull,
but on the inner road of faith.

Lord, in moments when I doubt you,
when questions cascade into my mind
and I can no longer believe without them,
grant me strength to trust,
not in the ability of my mind to comprehend you,
but in your mercy to receive me,
not in the sensitivity of my heart to feel you,
but in your promise to never leave me,
not in the light of a thousand suns,
but in the dark night of faith;
Lord, I believe. Help thou my unbelief.

Amen.

4

Jesus Meets His Loving Mother

Preaching in Galilee and told of the presence of his mother and brothers, Jesus said, "Who is my mother and my brother?" It is not an expression of indifference, but an acknowledgement that in the economy of the Kingdom there are no distinctions, no hierarchies of concern, only the response of self-giving love that is offered to all.

Lord, for those whom love has drawn to the road
 this day,
there are no nails to crucify their bodies,
nor spears to pierce their sides,
but yet a sword will pierce their souls
as it pierced the soul of Mary,
and it will feel like nothing so much as it feels like
 dying.

My brothers and sisters of the Way,
do not be afraid of my death;
it is my Exodus, a journey to a promised land,
a pulling of roots from this world

and a casting of them into the bottomless depths
of our Father's mystery.
What is perishable will become imperishable,
what is mortal will become immortal,
what is sown in humiliation will be raised in glory.

My mothers and fathers of the Way,
do not be afraid of my death,
for though our hands will not touch
and our bodies never again know the warmth of
    an embrace,
yet will we know a closeness
that cannot be crucified.
We will share a peace
that cannot be shattered by the baying crowd.
We will know love . . . for love does not die,
it is not diminished by absence.

Amen.

5

Simon Helps Jesus Carry His Cross

Simon of Cyrene was made to carry the cross. He was seized from the crowd that lined the road. His was the burden of necessity, not discipleship. He did not ask to be drawn into the events of that fateful day; he was just there, in the wrong place at the wrong time. Those who walk the Way of the Cross, however, will often find themselves giving thanks for the anonymous strangers who, unwittingly drawn into a life that is not theirs, have, for a little while, lifted the burden from their backs.

Lord, I chose to walk this Way with you,
to feel the weight of pain and suffering upon my
  back,
and bear the burden of other people's lives.
For Simon, there was no such choice:

an innocent bystander implicated in my freedom,
a stranger with whom I am inextricably bound,
a victim of chance
whom fate made the victim of my destiny.
Lord, thank you for the anonymous strangers:
those who support, comfort, and hold me

John Elliston

as I care for others,
those who encourage me with a smile
or a word of praise,
those who confirm, simply by their presence,
my commitment to the path I have chosen.
Give me grace to accept them
as they lift the cross from my back,
so that my belief that you have given them to me
may be greater than the guilt I feel at involving them,
and the joy with which I receive them
may be stronger than my sadness
at inflicting my pain upon them.

Amen.

6

Veronica Wipes the Face of Jesus

St. Veronica was a woman of Jerusalem who in legend is said to have offered her head-cloth to Christ to wipe the blood and sweat from his face on the Via Dolorosa, the Way of the Cross. When he returned it to her, his features were impressed upon it. She was there to comfort him, but from within his suffering, he, the comforted, gave comfort to her, the comforter.

Lord, the suffering that is mine on this journey
   none can share,
but there is a suffering of those who watch:

those who stand by in anger and helplessness,
those who are lost in the blind alley of "whys?,"
those who feel betrayed and cheated
as they are forced to surrender to death
that which they love,
and I know that their suffering is neither less
   intense,
nor less real,
nor less hard to bear,
than my own.

John Elliston

Grant to me the courage on my journey of pain
not to become indifferent to those who,
in small, insignificant ways,
reach out to comfort me,
who offer all that they have in touch, in words,
in the constancy of their presence,
and, though they stand on the outside
   of my experience,
remain and do not abandon me.

Lord, as you left your mark upon the life of
   Veronica,
may I be strong enough as I walk this Way
to leave my mark on those who comfort me,
so that when my journey is over, and my presence
   no more,
my smile, my word of hope, or my love for them,
may be imprinted on their memory
   and ease their grief.

Amen.

7

Jesus Falls a Second Time

*Thou who hast made me see many sore troubles
wilt revive me again; from the depths of the earth
thou wilt bring me up again. Thou wilt increase
my honor, and comfort me again.*

Psalm 71:20–21

Lord, I fear the dark valley,
the lonely voyage to my body's death;
I know it must come, but I fear the empty dream,
I fear the road that leads nowhere,
I fear crucifixion lest there be no resurrection.

Lord, pinned to the earth of failure
  by the weight of the cross,
I have fallen into hopelessness,
a barren landscape where the future is dark,
where life is meaningless,
and my daily work
is like plowing an unyielding field.
Grant me, in this moment,
the courage to hold on to what I know,
the wisdom to not become swamped by the negative
without taking due regard for the positive,
and a patience that is prepared to wait

for the first light of dawn,
though it may be long in coming.
Help me to recognize that though, through pain,
I feel your absence,
what I feel cannot cancel
what I have known in times of joy:

the certainty of faith at my baptism,
the joy of worshipping with your people,
the celebration of communion when,
in rare and blessed moments,
I felt at one with you.
May these become the strength that lifts me to my feet,
the inspiration to once again take the cross upon my back.

Amen.

8

Jesus Meets the Weeping Women

To weep endlessly for others will in the end comfort
no one. But we should not therefore be ashamed of
our tears. They are the outer signs of inner reality—
they speak when tongues fall silent.

Lord, as I look into the women's tear-filled eyes,
I recognize myself where they now stand;
I have watched helplessly events that I could not
   control,
I have wept as, in sympathy,
I have grieved for strangers,
I have cried silently, powerless,
before the suffering of those I love.
Now it is my Gethsemane, my Via Dolorosa,
   my Golgotha,
and I must eat the bread of compassion,
I must drink the wine of their tears—
   and be filled . . .
for it is all there is.

Lord, thank you for the gift of compassion,
for the ability of love to look beyond itself,
for the sensitivity to touch another's pain,

John Elliston

and for the consolation
that genuinely strives for understanding and
so lends strength to the consoled.
Grant me the humility
to accept the compassion of all those strangers
who meet me on the way;

those who, through their tears,
walk with me,
those who, powerless as they feel,
will not surrender me,
those who are strong enough to not let me die alone.

Holy Father, on the voyage of personal pain
it is easy to become angry
and to chide the weeping women and to reject
   their tears;
help me then, Lord, to recognize the cost of tears,
that to weep for me in my darkness
means that they too are in darkness.

Amen.

9

Jesus Falls a Third Time

From the depths of his pain, the Old Testament writer Job puts God on trial. The transcript of the case is long and the line of questioning is complex. It could all be summarized, however, by the question in the eyes of a young victim of terrorism, "Why?"

Lord, the Way of the Cross
still humiliates people before it destroys them,
cruelly and without discrimination
taking away dignity from those who, before the journey,
bore the image of their Creator with pride
but who now, lacerated by the scourge,
and staggering under the weight of the cross they carry,
fall broken into the dark cavern of questioning despair.

Lord, when I question the path I have chosen,
when pain and exhaustion overtake my body,
and I cannot sustain the pace of belief,
when I lose my sense of direction,
and every lonely step
draws me deeper into hopelessness,

grant me to recognize that I question you because I
   love you,
that I rail at you because of fear,
and I doubt you
because I believe that somewhere in the darkness
you are there.

Amen.

10

Jesus Is Stripped of His Garments

For Teilhard de Chardin, as for the apostle Paul, flesh and blood are the garments of humanity with which God, in the beginning, clothes us, and which, through the aging of our bodies, and ultimately in death, he removes in order to draw us to himself.

Lord, death is at work within me,
the unseen march of time
leaves marks upon my body
and still more upon my mind,
imperceptibly stripping me of youth,
of strength, of faculties,
and so drawing me to that fearful day
when the body that from the earth came into the world,
must to the earth return.

Grant me grace, Holy Father,
to accept the loss that aging brings,
and to neither be resentful of youth's power,
angry at lost opportunities,
nor exhausted in pointless battles with time.
May I possess an inner contentment

John Elliston

and a quiet peace in the face of the inevitable,
and even as my body is stripped of youth,
may I still know a faith that is strong enough
to realize both the beauty and potential
of the time that remains.

Lord, there are those who are stripped of their
   garments
long before it is time for their final rest;
those robbed of the health of their body
by disease or wasting;
those from whom society has taken all self-worth;
Alzheimer's children
whose bodies are sepulchres of minds
long since departed.
Help me to believe that all that they have lost
has already been gathered into your love,
and that if I too must walk that way,
you will never desert me.

Amen.

11

Jesus Is Nailed to the Cross

The curse of death is its finality. Whatever lies beyond it, whether darkness or light, means the end of life as we have always known it. Before the final surrender, there is always a final battle.

Lord, you entered into human weakness,
you felt our pain,
stood beside us in our dereliction.
The marks of the nails are still in your hands,

> the stigmata of love,
> the scars of your sacrifice,
> the perpetual sign of human frailty;

these you have taken into eternity, and made them
  holy.

Lord, it is now my body that feels pain,
it touches every part, consuming all my energy,
stealing my humanity by slow, fearful degrees,
allowing neither the retreat of my mind
nor the release of my spirit.
It hurts so much that I can think of nothing else,
except how alone I feel in this body of flesh,

John Elliston

how abandoned to the mercy of tears,
how I just can't take any more.
Lord, grant me grace,
so that when pain fills my body
and my mind becomes the arena
for a lonely battle for final release,
mine will not be a cry of forsakenness,
but a reaching after Christ,
who in the torment of the Cross
has walked the Way before me,
and by the miracle of faith will hold my hand.

Amen.

12

Jesus Dies upon the Cross

Death is an enemy, the last enemy according to the apostle Paul. But death is also a friend; the death that Francis of Assisi called "kind and gentle" is almost motherly as it draws us home to the Father.

Lord, I have walked the way with you
for this moment alone,
this dark moment of death,
the last healing of all,
when the weight is lifted from my shoulders,
and I give to you, my Father, the life I owe.
"Father, into your hands I commend my spirit."

Lord, as I approach the moment of my dying,
grant me the courage to let go of this life in faith,
believing that death does not have the final word,
believing that through death
   humanity is transfigured,
believing that you, the God of my pilgrimage,
will receive me as a Father receives a prodigal son.
May I know that nothing in love is lost,
that all things are held in grace,
and that in my death you are drawing me to yourself.
Holy Father, as I die,

John Elliston

may I know, so far as it is possible to know,
your mercy,
your acceptance, and your peace,
and for the rest,
grant to me, my Father, the strength to trust you.

Amen.

13

Jesus Is Taken Down from the Cross

Now there was a man named Joseph from the Jewish town of Arimathea. . . . This man went to Pilate and asked for the body of Jesus. Then he took it down and wrapped it in a linen shroud, and laid him in a rock-hewn tomb, where no one had ever yet been laid. Luke 23:50–53

Lord, it is hands of flesh and blood
that must receive my body in death,
a corpse that has been my home,
marked by passion,
scarred by the violence of pain,
yet still warm with love, companionship, and
   kindness.

Lord, though it is but a sign of my humanity,
I cannot leave my flesh without tears,
I cannot let go without regret,
I cannot abandon those I love
to the deprivation and emptiness
of bereavement and not know pain;
for I have loved the glory of your creation,
I have felt pleasure in the life you have given,
I have eaten the precious bread of sorrow and joy,

John Elliston

I have drunk the wine of laughter and pain,
I have known the mystery of loneliness and fear.
Gracious God,
though the things of earth are now pale
in the light of your presence,
I cannot forget my pilgrimage through time,
for it was in traveling the path of humanity
I fell in love with you.

Amen.

14

Jesus Is Laid in the Tomb

> He whom we love and lose is no longer where
> he was before. He is now wherever we are.
> *John Chrysostom, fourth-century*
> *bishop of Constantinople*

The most profound silence of all is the silence of death. Nothing is heard—no words, no breath, no heartbeat. The body is still, cold, lifeless. It is at peace. This can be very reassuring when the death has been slow in coming or painful. Those who remain see that the struggle for life has ended, that the crucifixion of disease, or tears, or age is over, and that the body, which in life was a person's home, has been mysteriously transformed into a symbol of eternal rest.

Lord, the tomb is a place of silence.
Within, there is the silence of death, cold, hard,
uncompromising in the harshness of its reality.
Without, there is the silence of grief
as it struggles to find words to articulate loss.
Beyond, there is the silence of eternity,
the mystery of your being,
which defies all language but love.

John Elliston

Lord, grant me to know
that the silence that only love can interpret
embraces both the silence of death and the silence
 of grief,
that in my death I will not be separated
from those who love and mourn me,
but that as love bound us in this life,
so we will remain forever bound,
for love never ends.

Amen.

15

The Resurrection

In the art of the Eastern Church, the resurrection is often illustrated by a picture of Christ climbing out of the tomb, drawing Adam by the hand. Adam, the first man, is a representative figure, standing for all humanity. The picture is a reminder that between life and resurrection lies our death. Yet death holds no fear. Death is the call of love, the voice of the risen Christ, drawing us from this life into the life to come, from the pilgrimage of flesh to the glory of resurrection.

Lord, there will be a day of homecoming,
when the dark glass of this world
will be shattered to reveal the world to come,
when the ravages of age, and pain, and death
  will fall away,
and when all that by faith I have sought in this life
will be as real as the body
into which Thomas placed his hand.

Give me courage to go forward boldly,
relying on all that through Christ
you achieved on the third day,
so that when death threatens

John Elliston

and the earth shudders in travail,
I will face it as one who goes to meet his Lord.

Glory be to the Father, and to the Son, and to the
  Holy Spirit.
As it was in the beginning, is now, and ever shall be,
world without end.

Amen.

www.ingramcontent.com/pod-product-compliance
Lightning Source LLC
Chambersburg PA
CBHW052038070526
44584CB00020B/3150